This book belongs to:

____

95235304R00066

Made in the USA
Middletown, DE
25 October 2018